CONTENT

ACKNOWLEDGEMENT

The executant will usually be the person who deliberately decides to put things into proper perspective.

Although active citizenship, a concept underpinned by intercultural diversity, is meant to be a voluntary act within the society, the adverse is the usual experience in most communities.

In my short life, I have come across quite a number of executants, who not only mentored me but also assisted me in the realization of my goals and ambition.

Given that this book cannot contain all their names, I have decided to say thank you to you all.

You have all worked together to make my life what it is today.

Above all my sincere gratitude goes to the big GOD who has kept me standing.

Kudos to my spouse, my family members and all of you for the value you have added to my life

The Missing Child

At about 10 am one beautiful Tuesday morning I was on my way back from the seaside where I had gone for a quiet time when one young lady ran towards me demanding to know whether I had sighted a child on the street.

Having walked through the whole length of that street, my answer was a frantic NO!

Given that we were right in front of the gate that leads to our local Educate Together School coupled with my assumption that such environment will interest children, I simply advised her to check the school campus.

That impromptu conversation changed the course of my journey for the day as I Immediately enlisted in the search party.

With deep concern, I zealously went through the nook and cranny of the estate looking for a child whose gender, colour, nationality, look, age or stature I never had the time to find out.

All that mattered to me then, was that the missing child must be found!

Notwithstanding the dichotomy between us; although we are both Irish, I am a naturalized citizen; we were determined to fish out the child.

This is exactly what being an active citizen represents.

It entails the coming together of individuals from diverse cultural and ethnic background for a communal cause or activity.

Reminiscent of my childhood days, I vividly remembered my late mother's usual slogan, "You only have two eyes but two hundred eyes are watching your back".

How nice would it be to have that many people vigilantly watching over various apprehensions within our community?

How nice will it be? That means less concern for security and safety.

A lady I once asked what role she was playing in a new movie she was involved in sometimes ago introduced an unusual word to me when I enquired about her.

"I am a Chaperone," she said.

A Chaperone? So when will your scene come up? I pondered further in ignorance.

It was then that I found out that the Chaperone neither appear on a script nor play any role in a movie.

Although Chaperones always eat and dine with the actors, they are never seen on the big screen.

An Active citizen can sometimes be likened to a Chaperone. They may not be prevalent in the eyes of the public yet they do extra ordinary exploits behind the scene!

However, active citizenship transcends beyond merely watching from the background rather, there is an active participatory dimension involved.

Active citizenship is all about peaceful communal living! A situation where all the members of the community come together for a common goal that addresses the worries and anxieties of one another in love.

Promoting this culture will usually create a harmonious atmosphere devoid of the ills and decadences existing within our society.

It brings an end to the hate game and its resultant effect currently phenomenal on our airwaves as members of the community proffer solutions that will adequately fit their environment. A case of the home grown solution to the unique consternations.

As I continued my search for the missing child within the vicinity of the local shopping centre, the lady suddenly showed up again.

You could guess what was running through my mind as I anxiously ran towards her.

Yes, you are right. "Did you find the child?" was the only question on my lips.

Her expression confirmed my fears as she said, "No".

Eager to continue with the hunt, I asked her for a detailed description of the missing child.

"What age is the child you are looking for?" I probed further.

It was then I realized that she was just another Active Citizen!

She overheard someone who was looking for a child while shopping around the locality and joined in the search party.

Imagine what would happen If I had told someone who had gone ahead to tell some few other people?

We would have formed a formidable community child rescue force brought together by a common purpose.

Another Man's Poison

"One man's meat is another man's poison", was the thought that flashed through my mind sometimes ago while watching an interesting short film.

A group of company directors in Europe had called a meeting where some contract terms were to be agreed and signed with some of their foreign partners.

They had prearranged the meeting to hold in one of the best hotels in town.

The top executives that will be representing the company had practiced several pitching techniques before arriving at the most appropriate.

They had prepared scripts with the detailed plan of how the day would go.

Unfortunately, the party had barely started eating when one of the foreigners stood up in anger, "Holy Cow?" she protested.

According to her, Cows are sacred. They are meant to be worshipped and not eaten by humans.

No sooner had they resolved the issue that the second partner began his protest too. "Do you mean that I have just eaten pork?" was all he said.

The short film ended by making us aware that both foreigners abandoned the meeting and the contract was never signed.

Why? Beef and Pork are good delicacies in Europe but they are forbidden in some parts of the world.

Active citizenship is one of the five factors underpinning intercultural diversity.

It is perhaps the first gap that must be closed to foster a peaceful coexistence within any community.

Particularly where there is an iota of intercultural diversity amongst its citizenry.

The four other gaps being, social inclusion, anti-racism, peacebuilding and conflict resolution.

<table>
<tr><td>Active Citizenship</td><td>Social Inclusion</td><td>Anti Racism</td><td>Conflict Resolution</td></tr>
</table>

Intercultural Diversity

The European hosts could have probably prevented the chaos that ensued during the meeting had they been aware of this first gap.

Closing this gap would have exposed them to the visitors' cultural inclination and they would have averted the traumatic experience!

Intercultural diversity is a representation of a diverse population differentiated by individual culture.

An in-depth understanding of the diverse nature of culture is required to foster an enduring active citizenship.

What then is culture?

The representation of Professor Geert Hofstede of Maastricht University on cultural dimensions still remains the main authority on culture.

Illustrating culture with an onion bulb, Hofstede opined that culture revolves around values basically consisting of our rituals, heroes, and symbols.

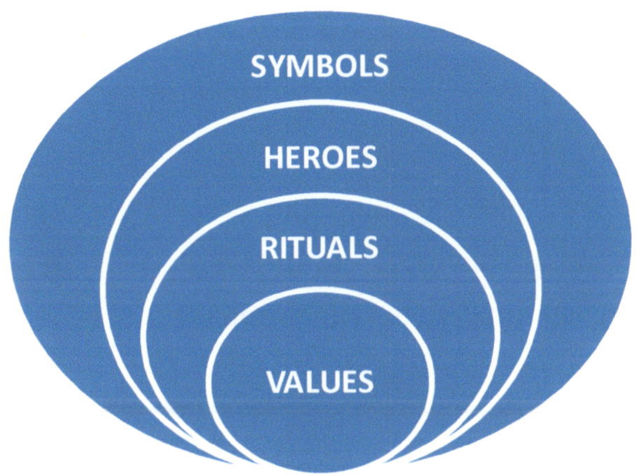

In deed, one will agree that culture is a true representation of not only what we value, but also our rituals, heroes, and symbols.

For instance, coming from a family of seven, it has was a norm that each member of the family will be entitled to two pieces of chicken and a bag of fries whenever we eat out in Kentucky Fried Chicken.

One of us got used to this values that he couldn't help expressing his astonishment the first time he noticed some little child devour five pieces of chicken within a matter of minutes.

This is a typical example of family values.

In the same vein, one's value system could be premised on individual, societal or national inclination.

Hofstede went further to create a contextual continuum of different cultures that are quite useful for messages and communication.

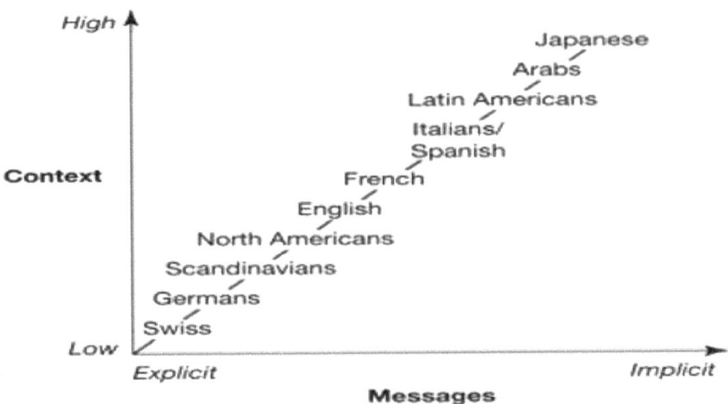

He then devised a six-dimensional continuum to support his illustration.

1) Individualist / Collectivist: This is the degree to which an individual's beliefs and actions are independent of collective thoughts and actions.
   While an individualistic society encourages the pursuit of personal goals, a collectivist society operates in groups.

2) Masculinity/Femininity: Relating to the level of assertiveness within a culture, a feminist culture is less assertive. It is the vice versa for a masculine society.

3) Uncertainty avoidance: This is concerned with the degree to which a society feels threatened by ambiguous situations. Societies that are rated high on uncertainty avoidance have highly structured working environments.

4) Power distance: This notion is determined by how a society accepts the idea that power is to be distributed unequally through hierarchical distinctions.

5) Time Perspective: Divided into Long and Short term perspective, a long-term culture focuses on the distant future while a culture that embraces short-term culture thinks only of their immediate needs.

6) Indulgence / Restraint: This classification assumes that while some cultures prefer instant gratification, other cultures operate a strict social norm.

The Emeritus Professor Geert Hofstede conducted this research based on IBM staff survey of 72 countries and 20 languages and concluded that

"Culture is more often a source of conflict than of synergy."

In his opinion, "Cultural differences are a nuisance at best and often a disaster"

Taking a cue from the Jeff Sutherland, a co-creator of "Scrum", I am of the opinion that culture revolves around five basic concepts.

These are cultural traditions, previous experiences and genetic heritage. Closely followed by its analysis, synthesis and newly discovered facts or information.

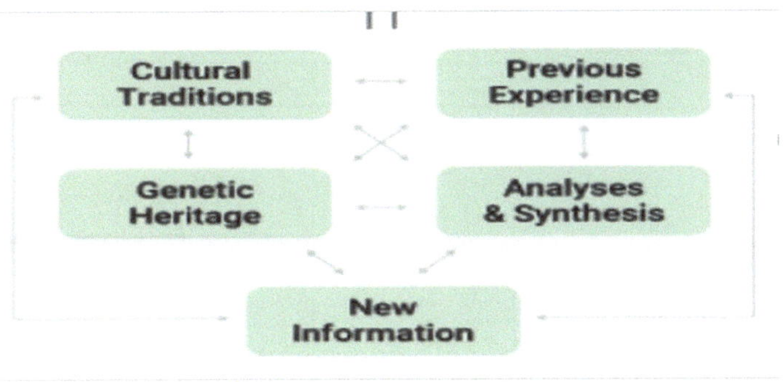

Active citizenship is all about people coming together for the good of their local communities. They could organize campaigns to reduce obesity in the community, maintain a street, educate young people or fight some other social menaces.

The separate Chair

Uncle, I said I want the square orange bowl today! Retorted Loamy, one of the very smart tots that usually arrived early enough for the breakfast club daily.

The second of the three siblings from the same parent, her dad usually dropped her off, along with Tommy her big sister and Dan their little brother in haste, before quickly dashing out to work.

Tommy had settled down with one of the orange bowls while Dan simply snacked on a banana from the second orange bowl.

Knowing that the crèche only had two orange bowls, which are being used by his siblings we had no choice but to persuade Loamy that her breakfast will be served her using another bowl. The only alternative was that she will take turns after either of them.

"Will you try out this new pink bowl?" I asked. "No Uncle! Uncle No! She bluntly refused.

What about this purple one? I asked. "Uncle No!" replied Loamy.

"Oh, I just bought a pink and orange bowl, will you try that?" I asked after a while. "No, Uncle, No, No" she replied again!

In contrast to her other siblings, Loamy not only knew what she wanted, but when she wanted it. She has always called the shot.

None of the crèche staff could say exactly what happened to the orange bowl overnight.

What is so special about the orange square bowl? Nothing! It is just like any other fanciful utensils bought for the children attending our crèche.

Did you say crèche?

Yes, we used to run a crèche and child care facility some years back. This was because we had to be around one of our children who had just been discharged from the intensive care unit of the hospital.

This was to enable us regularly administer what is known as nasogastric (NG) intubation, NG Tube for short, on the child as he could only be fed through his nostrils with the aid of a tube.

Were we to classify Loamy's culture according to Hofstede Dimensions, she will be on the highest spectrum of the masculinity/feminism continuum.

Loamy knew what she wanted and nothing could stop her from getting whatsoever she desired.

Having persuaded Loamy to no avail, I ordered that she should be sent to a separate chair.

"Sorry Uncle, sorry!" The poor little girl exclaimed, after a long while.

"Sorry, sorry, sorry Uncle", Loamy said again.

Loamy's predicament clearly depict a graphic picture of the second gap. Social exclusion!

This anecdote is required to explain social inclusion, the opposite of social exclusion.

Although Loamy sat on the separate chair for just a few seconds, her emotions could not be controlled until she made me order her personal square orange bowl online.

Members of the society that are socially excluded will often consider themselves as being shut up in a separate chair. Due to no fault of their own.

The separate chair may cause such people to be quiet but this is just a temporary panacea.

Not being able to partake in what other people derive pleasure from will usually be considered as bullying, and this may ultimately lead to some mental health issues.

Where an adult is constantly made to sit in separate seat, it could easily lead to resentfulness, which over time, may manifest as what is known as cognitive dissonance in Psychology.

According to Leon Festinger, cognitive dissonance could be described as a condition involving contradictory behaviours, attitudes or beliefs.

The effect of such contradiction usually engender feelings of discomfort that eventually culminates in the deliberate fine-tuning of one's disposition, belief system and attitude in order to lessen or eliminate the discomfort.

Members of the community who have experienced such exclusion could force themselves into a transient compliance mode like Loamy.

The fact that her personal square orange bowl was ordered restored her cognitive consonance thereby eliminating retaliative attitudes that could ensue thereafter; while also proactively maintaining the safety of her fellow toddlers.

Given that individuals will generally seek consistency among their cognitions; beliefs and opinions; attempts aimed at eliminating the dissonance is a prerogative.

Cognitive consistency and dissonance vary between cultures, traditions and ethnicity and as such a clear understanding of the underlying intercultural diverse society portend to close this gap.

Promoting interaction amongst different communities by way of education can also help achieve the elimination of this gap.

Community with a well-developed active citizenship competencies will obviously be on a better pedestal to eliminate violent extremism, terrorist attacks and other insurrection and insurgencies in no time.

Coffee Morning

"Can you please try and attend the coffee morning at the children's school this morning?" asked my loving wife early one morning.

The children were just resuming school after the long summer break and they were very excited that they will see their friends and teachers again.

"This doesn't fit into my plan for the day." I thought within me.

"I would have attended the meeting myself but for the 8 am call I have this morning", she continued.

Still keeping numb, "How can I go and sit down for a cup of coffee or whatever it is so called early this morning?" I thought to myself.

Sensing my reluctance she changed her tone of voice and said, "a lot of parents were at the last meeting and we were out of the place in less than 30 minutes."

"After all you could be stuck in traffic for that long", she continued.

"Do you really have to persuade me before I attend a meeting that concerns my children?" I exclaimed.

That was after she had taken her time to explain to me that "Coffee Morning" was just another fancy word coined by the school to encourage parents to get together and deliberate in a relaxed atmosphere.

Recalling "Hofstede contextual continuum of differing culture", you would probably rate my disposition towards the appellation "Coffee Morning" as a high contextual culture.

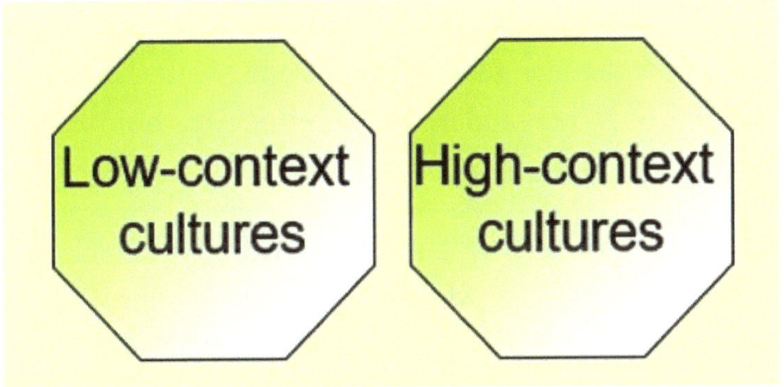

Dropping off the kids as I would normally do, I parked the car in a safe place across the road and proceeded to the venue of the "Coffee Morning". I was quite surprise to discover that a whole bunch of multi-ethnic people were already there.

That was when I realized why the school was called "ETNS", short for Educate Together National School.

Although it was the first time I will attend such a meeting, I was warmly welcomed and thereafter ushered to a seat.

The particular parent that sat next to me happened to be a long-standing member of the Parents Teachers Association of the school and for the very first time, he told me how they had come together to start the school.

Unlike the magnetic force where like poles repel each other, like humans tend to attract one another creating a dichotomy of gender, races, ethnicity, colour and age, to mention a few.

Race is a very sensitive issue and we all have a bit of racism in us. The simple solution is this, "Stop feeding it".

What we feed grows! Refusing to nurture the small element of racism in one will put it in a starvation mode.

I sat next to a man from a totally different race and made up my mind to starve the thing that was telling me we are different. That is how to close that third gap!

Although I was repeatedly saying "pardon me" on several occasions, I patiently listened to the man's story.

Diverse ethnicity demands not only specialised communication skills, but also varying tone of voice in addition to many other innate dimensions.

The only common factor between us was the fact that our children attend the same school and will probably have similar issues to deal with.

It was there that I had the rare privilege of learning that "ETNS" is a child of convenience brought about as a result of Intercultural Diversity.

Stereotypes and biases can also engender the cancer called racism.

Someone once told me that I should never generalize from specifics. That is true to itself and adopting such philosophy will no doubt close this gap.

The fact that people from different cultural or ethnic background behave in a particular way does not necessarily imply that everyone from such background will exhibit the same characteristic.

Tweaking the circumstance a little bit may result in a whole new discovery that closes the racism gap.

Understanding what triggers racism is also a good way to prevent racial intolerance.

Deep-seated fears in people may be one of such. The fear of not knowing the orientation, culture, attitude, and belief of the other party can in itself breed some racist action.

We should all work towards promoting equality in opportunities as well as agreeing on reprisal for discriminatory activities.

The "Coffee Morning" turned out be an event that celebrates multiculturalism. It is another remedy that closes gap no 3.

Organising deliberate multi-ethnicity functions and events to foster collaborations leading to open communication that reduces prejudices is another good device.

Promoting openness to diversity will also build the tolerance level of the incumbent race which will ultimately result in the thoughtful and affective empathy towards the victim.

The Dinner

I still vividly remember the days when we used to travel out of town to work.

Our usual routine was to wake up very early in the morning to prepare the children for school and also get their meals ready in time to hit the road before the typically early traffic.

Our custom was to drop off the older children in the local school while the younger ones drive with us to Dublin City for a full day crèche.

I was dropping them off on one of the days when the teacher who came to meet me in the car requested to know if my children had dinner before coming to school that morning.

Dinner? I asked, bewildered.

Driving down the motorway, I began to ponder on what the teacher meant.

Was she referring to their dinner last night? Or was that was a slip of tongue?

I shrugged off the thoughts as I battled through the heavy traffic and totally forgot about that conversation until the next morning.

Dropping off the children the next day, I deliberately waited for the teacher so as to patiently listen to what she would say.

Obviously, her statement sounded as if she was reading from a prepared script.

"Good morning, did you enjoy your dinner?" She asked.

I couldn't help but wonder if dinner was served early in the morning in that teacher's house.

Was she referring to their breakfast? Or is breakfast known as dinner in this part of the world?

The conversation gradually became a part of me and by the time I would drop off my children at the end of the week, I had found myself telling them to ensure that they eat their dinner before leaving the house.

My experience with the teacher is a real-life example of conflicting cultures.

It is the implicit or explicit emotional frustration between persons of different cultures over perceived incompatible values, norms or orientation in a communication situation.

When it comes to intercultural conflict, the grey area is usually a function of one's rituals, heroes, and symbols.

I have always known the first meal of the day as breakfast whereas, in the teacher's culture, the biggest meal of the day will be considered to be dinner.

Standard over form, a crucial concept in Accounting, is a term I will employ to explain how one can easily resolve this type of conflict.

According to my Accounting 101 lecturer, you may get to an office to find out that the man who answers telephone calls is referred to as the secretary; whereas such person is known as the personal assistance in your office.

Rather than get confused, look at the job function, which is the standard and ignore the form.

The standard in the case of my children's dinner is the meal.

You may choose to call your meal whatever name you prefer. The obvious fact is that it is still a meal.

People of varying cultural orientation value things differently.

Closing the conflict management gap entails resolving the valence between the opposing cultures.

An indicator of the emotional value associated with a stimulus, this fourth gap could be closed using positive valence.

One may also consider employing one of these four conflict management strategies.

 Depending on the level of assertiveness and cooperation, a person may reach a compromise by either avoiding or accommodating the negative behavior.

They may also choose to compete or collaborate on the high assertiveness continuum.

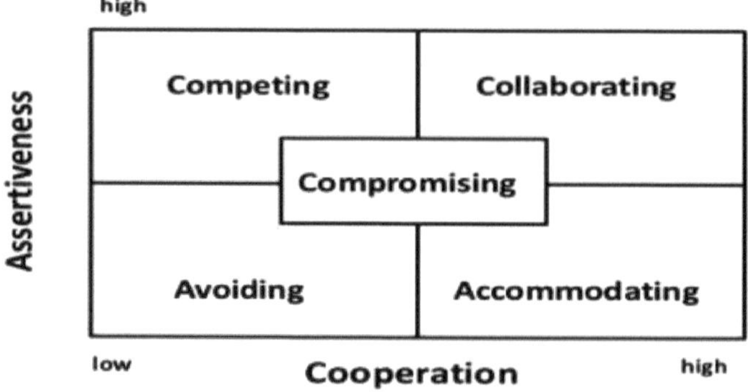

Happiness is now

Growing up as a little child, I used to attend a Sunday school where we sing one particular song almost every week.

We are H-A-P-P-Y, We are H-A-P-P-Y

And so we are, we are sure we are,

We are H-A-P-P-Y, Happy.

It feels good to be happy. When you are happy offence does not matter to you.

A happy person does not notice insults nor get begrudged. Happy people will usually exhibit a kind of confidence that cannot be found in any other person.

Some people who were once asked what will make them happy responded differently.

While some believe that winning the Lotto will make them happy, some other people were of the opinion that promotion and more successes are the antidote that can boost their level of happiness.

However, thinking that happiness is a destination is a total fallacy!

It is now! Be happy now! Happiness is now! Not when you reach a desired destination. Desires will always be there.

The fundamental of Economics says that, "Human wants are insatiable."

While studying for a master's degree in Managerial Psychology I learned that Psychological researchers believe that happiness is life experience marked by a preponderance of positive emotion.

The feelings of happiness and thoughts of satisfaction with life are two prime components of subjective well-being

Philosophers also believe that happiness is one of the keys to prosperity. In fact, the term "happiness" is synonymous with "luck" in most European languages.

According to Friedrich Nietzsche, "happiness is the feeling that power increases"

Socrates, who lived in 450 BC believes that "The secret of happiness is not found in seeking more, but in developing the capacity to enjoy less"

He also opined that happiness doesn't come from external rewards or accolades but from the private, internal success people bestow upon themselves.

The account of Joseph in the Bible begs to support this view.

Naturally one would assume that Joseph was discharged from the prison because of his God-given ability to interpret dreams.

However, the twist to this dimension lie in the fact, that it was recorded that Joseph noticed that the baker and the butler were not happy.

This signifies that Joseph was a happy man, even while serving a jail term for a crime he never committed.

Plato, who also lived in 4th century BC said "The man who makes everything that leads to happiness depends upon himself, and not upon other men has adopted the very best plan for living happily"

Happiest people live a "balanced" life, working a little over seven hours per day, exercising frequently, enjoying cooked meals five times a week, and seeing their friends once per week, reinforced Einstein.

HAPPINESS METRIC

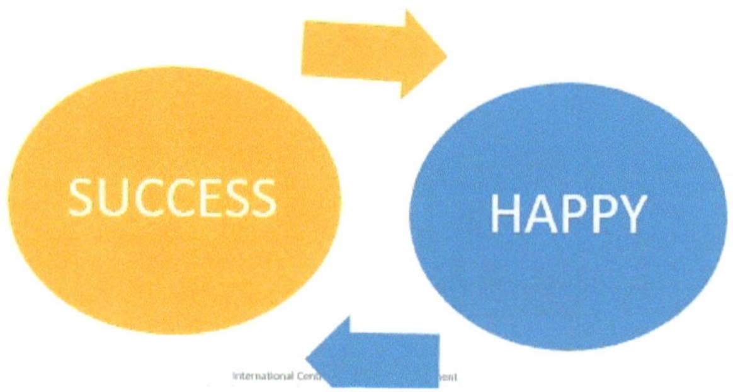

Time will not permit us to talk about Albeit Einstein's Theory of Happiness but it is pertinent to note that while the autographed photo of Albert Einstein with his tongue out was sold at auction for $125,000, the note bearing his "Theory of Happiness" sold at an auction for $1.56 million.

His take on happiness is that it leads to behaviors that often produce further success in work, relationships, and health.

These successes result in part from a person's positive affect.

"A calm and modest life brings more happiness than the pursuit of success combined with constant restlessness." He concluded.

"Happiness depends upon ourselves", says Aristotle, who lived in Ancient Greece sometimes around 300 BC.

Aristotle's definition of happiness is that "happiness depends on ourselves more than anybody else.

He enshrines happiness as a central purpose of human life and a goal in itself

Conclusively, the following reflects the thoughts of various Scholars on happiness.

Aristotle argued that virtue is achieved by maintaining the mean, which is the balance between two excesses.

"The more man meditates upon good thoughts, the better will be his world and the world at large" — Confucius, lived in China around 500 BC.

"The greatest blessings of mankind are within us and within our reach. A wise man is content with his lot, whatever it may be, without wishing for what he has not" — Seneca, born in Hispania in 4 BC.

"If you are depressed you are living in the past. If you are anxious you are living in the future. If you are at peace you are living in the present" — Lao Tzu, 600 BC in China.

"Happiness is like a butterfly; the more you chase it, the more it will elude you, but if you turn your attention to other things, it will come and sit softly on your shoulder" said Henry David Thoreau in 1817 in Massachusetts.

References

Festinger, L. (1957). *A Theory of cognitive dissonance*. Stanford, CA: Stanford University Press.

Hofstede, G. (1980) Culture's Consequences, McGraw-Hill, New York.

Sutherland, J. (2014) Scrum: The Art of Doing Twice the Work in Half the Time. Random House Business Books, London.